THE LITTLE CLUBHOUSE ON STEAMSHIP WHARF

DEDICATION

On Mission Bay, in the quiet time before the motorboats, the skiers, the windsails and the sailboats come, you can find any number of San Diego Rowing Club members on the bay. For an hour or so, they row their shells, feeling the water run beneath them.

It is a tranquil time for both the rowers and the club, in contrast to the exciting time when it was recognized as one of the most powerful rowing clubs in the country. On the edge of a rowing renaissance, the club will again be known and popular.

This book is dedicated to those who rowed when the sport declined and to those who have kept the club going, refusing to let it end.

THE LITTLE CLUBHOUSE ON STEAMSHIP WHARF

San Diego Rowing Club 1888-1983

by
Patricia A. Schaelchlin

★   ★   ★

Cover Sketches by Robert Miles Parker

Rand Editions
Leucadia, California

Editor: Elizabeth Rand
Book Design: Rosemary Christensen
Cover design: Justine Wenman
Published by Rand Editions
P.O. Box 2610
Leucadia, California 92024

EPIGRAPH

For the past nine years, I have rowed about, during a good part of the summer, on fresh or salt water.... (I row in) my own particular water sulky, a "Skeleton" or "shell" race boat, twenty-two feet long, with huge outriggers, which boat I pull with ten foot sculls, alone of course, as it holds but one, and tips him out if he does not mind what he is about. In this I glide around the Back Bay, down the stream, up the Charles to Cambridge and Watertown, up the Mystic, around the wharves, in the wake of steamboats, which leave a swell after them delightful to rock upon. I linger under the bridges, those "caterpillar bridges," as my brother professor so happily called them, rub against the black sides of the old wood schooners; cool down under the overhanging sterns of some tall Indiaman, stretch across the Navy Yard where the sentinel warns me off the Ohio, just as if I should hurt her by lying in the shadow; then strike out into the harbor, where the water gets clear and the air smells of the ocean, till all at once, I remember, that if a west wind blows up of a sudden, I shall drift along past the islands, out of sight of the dear old State house, plate, tumbler knife and fork all waiting at home, but no chair drawn up at the table, all the dear people waiting, waiting, waiting, while the boat is sliding, sliding, sliding into the great desert, where there is no trees and no fountain. As I do not want my wreck to be washed up on one of the beaches in company with devil's aprons, bladder weeds, dead horseshoes, and bleached crab shells, I turn about and flap my long narrow wings for home. When the tide is running out swiftly, I have a splendid fight to get through the bridges, but always make it a rule to beat, though I have-been jammed up into pretty tight places at times, and was caught once between a vessel swinging around and the pier, until our bones (the boat's that is) cracked as if we had been in the jaws of a Behemoth. Then back to my moorings at the foot of the Common, off with the rowing dress, dash under the green translucent wave, return to the garb of civilization...."

Oliver Wendell Holmes,
From *The Autocrat of the Breakfast Table*

1890 Steamship Wharf with Chandler's Boathouse in upper left

THE SAN DIEGO ROWING CLUB

O n the evening of June 7, 1888, a group of thirteen men gathered at Steadman's Boathouse and formed the Excelsior Rowing Club. Steadman's boathouse was the logical place for the birth of the club, for most of the rowing activity originated here at this time.

R. B. Steadman was the "Proprietor of the San Diego Boathouse" located on the Pacific Coast Steamship Wharf at the foot of Fifth Avenue. He built and rented boats, and from his boathouse and with his boats all of the early races began. In 1887 he had built a new boathouse, leaving the old one because it was "too open to the prevailing winds."[1] It was in the old boathouse that the Excelsior Rowing Club began.

A name and a purpose

The name would be formally changed to the San Diego Rowing Club, chosen to more closely identify the club geographically in competition, on September 2, 1891.[2] The change had been proposed as early as January 1889, and it has remained the club's name to this day. (In 1921 the "San Diego Rowing and Athletic Club" name was suggested, but not adopted. The club unanimously voted to remain with their traditional name. Considered mergers with the Mission Valley Tennis Club would have resulted in a name change also, as a result of a move to Mission Bay in the 1950s, but the membership also voted against this. With tenacity, the club held to its identification throughout the years.)

The purpose of the club was to "... inaugurate a series of aquatic sports and to have regular drill days."[3] It was not

> ... formed for pecuniary profit, but is a social organization and is organized for the purpose of owning, controlling, and managing boats ... [and] maintaining a club house and bathing place and owning and leasing property necessary therefore.[4]

"The Father of Aquatic Sports in San Diego"

The club promoted San Diego water sports, competed locally and nationally, and became recognized as "The Father of Aquatic Sports in San Diego."

The organization of such a club had been talked about for many years. As early as February 1881 the *San Diego Union* reported: "We hope soon to report the formation of rowing and sailing clubs. We have the material here, both as to muscle, boat and harbors to make it a good thing in every way...."[5]

It was to remain the most prominent and influential men's club in San Diego for decades. Many of the members would sit in all levels of public office — and others were from the professional community — but it did not exclude anyone, for the club saw itself as a "truly plain club, minus frills, and offering fellowship and a stimulating life to its members."[6] There was no hierarchical distinction, as the members, the "gabooners," sunbathed together on the club's porch, discussing world affairs. They were all rowers, come together for the love of the sport, not because of their relative status.

It would be through the efforts of J. E. Peterson (who would be the first president) and Dave W. Dean (the first captain) that the club organized in 1888. Peterson, a plumber and gas fitter and a former Dolphin Club rower in San Francisco, acted as president only three months, leaving then to return to San Francisco. Dean, a carpenter and a champion oarsman, came to San Diego from San Francisco where he had been a member of the South End Rowing Club. Certainly all of the thirteen original members and the sixty charter members should be considered the founding members, for in the first five years of its existence members and officers came and left.

"Gabooners" on sun porch c. 1930

2

Structuring the club

The structure was patterned after the San Francisco Dolphin Club, and the constitution and bylaws guided them until the incorporation in 1895. In 1890, the club had been urged to incorporate, and again in June 1892 President E. J. Louis spoke of the necessity of having an identity:

> ... I assert that the club's condition will not be materially changed as an organization, except to be given an individuality, and vest it with the necessary power to transact its business as if it were an individual.

He told the members that as the club now functioned it was "... powerless in the eyes of the law." It would take another three years before the incorporation was finalized.

The bylaws called for a six-month term for the officers: president, vice-president, treasurer, secretary and captain. By January 1889, a recording secretary, a sergeant-at-arms, and first and second lieutenant offices had been added. The sergeant-at-arms office was eliminated in 1897, and the six-month term condition, within one year.

H. FORTBROOK

1 — F. Turner; 2 — Dr. McClearny; 3 — B. Johnson; 4 — I. Leszyn-
sky; 5 — H. Bagby; 6 — F. Henking; 7 — Dr. F. Carpenter; 8 — E.
Hickman; 9 — D. Seaman; 10 — H. Palmer; 11 Dr. T. McConkey;
12 — H. Kneale; 13 — F. Jackson; 14 — W. Dowd; 15 — T. Baker

Problems

The problems of the club in the first five years lay
essentially in the difficulty of keeping members, the changing
board of directors, and the establishing of suitable quarters for
storing and launching the boats . . . and because the spirited
young men didn't always agree.

There was great interest in the rowing club in 1888 and
many young men joined. The charter list was closed within
seven weeks. With each meeting, the membership list grew.
Keeping members, however, was a challenge.

By September 14, 1888, dues delinquency became an item
on the agenda and members were urged to come forward and
pay up. The financial secretary was instructed to "erase the
names of the members who were one month in arrears with
their subscription."

The officers had to deal with the problems of personal-
ities, and this stress led to a changing board of directors.
Peterson was succeeded by Vice-president H. R. Larrison (who
resigned a month later), followed by J. G. Decatur, who did
not run again in the January election. The 1890 board reflects a
constantly revolving set of officers, and in the next few years
the club suffered a declining interest in membership.

The board of directors election of 1893 saw a new
beginning, and the *San Francisco Chronicle* reported that a
"sinking fund" for improvements had been established.[7] In
1891, the club had moved to Chandler's boathouse, a short
distance from Steadman's. The club was in a condition "such
as to insure its becoming one of the foremost organizations of
its character on the Western coast."

One of the problems that faced the board was the location
for their quarters. Their first home was not suitable, probably
for the same reasons that Steadman had chosen to build a new
boathouse: the winds. The members were divided. Some
opted for better quarters with facilities for meeting while
others wished to remain at Steadman's boathouse, quite happy
with those quarters. By January 1889 the argument led to a
break that scarred the club for years.

Becoming known

The club did become well known, not just in the West but throughout the United States. By 1900 they had built a new clubhouse (still on the steamship wharf) and they would row from it for nearly seventy-nine years. They trained their teams to be the most competitive and successful in any association. The friction disappeared, and in 1895 after the annual meeting the members "adjourned" to Ingersoll's Ice Cream Parlor and "gave the club cheer (so) vigorously . . . 'San-dee-a-go — San-dee-a-go-go-go — San-dee-a-go-go' with the full lung power of twenty-five men . . . ."[8] It was the beginning.

Membership for women

In this time period, the regattas became a part of the rowing life. The races centered around social activities which included the women and children. Women had not been a part of the day-to-day events.

The Rowing Club Man, the club's news booklet, wrote in 1918:

> *Oftentimes, Miss or Missus S.D.R.C. admirer will say to herself, why can't we, too, have an all-joy place like the Rowing Club, to bask in the sunshine and splash in the refreshing waters of the bay? We all agree with them, that they should have such a place and here's suggesting to a real chance for some good-hearted, well-to-do to establish just such a club and thereby build an everlasting memorial for himself.*

The club had quartered four women's clubs in the early part of this century: The Columbias, Oceanids, Nereids and the La Sienas.[9] President J. S. Akerman, in 1902, remarked: "We need the room now used by the young ladies, but it would be unwise as well as discourteous to turn them out until they are provided for."

In 1922, the minutes read ". . . the practice of the ladies . . . changing their clothes at the clubhouse was agreed to be undesirable and strictly forbidden."[10]

In 1974, the first woman, Karen Proskauer, was given membership.

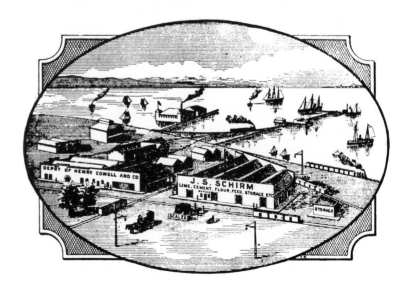

World Wars I and II

The focus of the club did not remain narrowly on rowing and competition, for during World War I and II many members entered the services, and some died in combat. The club supported its country and said so. In 1918 President Milton Epstein wrote:

In common with all other truly American institutions, the San Diego Rowing Club freely offered its entire resources to the government immediately after war was declared. Our telegram to the chief executive in this effect, and expressive of our confidence in the administration, was quickly followed by more substantial evidences of our attitude; practically one hundred and twenty of our members, or one-fifth of our entire membership, are actually wearing Uncle Sam's uniforms in all branches of the service; dozens of our older members are serving on the various committees that have to do with war financing, relief, and life service, and the club has purchased a substantial amount of Liberty Bonds. We are proud to think that we are really trying to "do our bit," and this policy will, of course, prevail during the present emergency, but there is yet another direction in which we can be of service, and that is one in which the help of every individual is required: we must back up our government in thought as well as deed, in the spirit as well as in the flesh;

therefore, we owe it as a duty to discourage all destructive criticism of the administration, and must, both as a club and as individuals absolutely refuse to tolerate anything that even remotely savors of an attitude not loyal American in the greatest and highest sense.[11]

The club played a very real part in World War II when again members served. The United States Navy requested and received permission to establish a listening post on the tip of Brennan Island (an island used by the club).[12] Through the war years, servicemen from the Naval Hospital used the club's facilities, and between September 1, 1942, and August 21, 1945, 15,486 men came to the club.[13] It was a time of reduced activity, for "during the duration of the war, it is impossible to use boats on the bay at night, to light Brennan Island or clubhouse porches."[14]

THE ANNUAL MEETING

of the members of the SAN DIEGO ROWING CLUB will be held at the Club House *Tuesday, May 8, 1923, at 7:30 o'clock p. m.*, for the election of officers for the ensuing year and the transaction of such other business as may properly come before it.

A Nominating Committee, consisting of Arthur Wright, Chairman; Cornelius Butler, Charles Lentz, Clarence Murray and Stephen Purcell, have named the following slate of candidates:

For President	E. B. GOULD, Jr.
For Vice-President	HARRY S. CLARK
For Treasurer	MERALD HUNTER
For Secretary	H. D. AUSTIN
For Captain	R. F. BARTHELMESS
For Captain	ARNHOLT SMITH
For First Lieutenant	HARLEY KNOX
For First Lieutenant	GLEN REMINGTON
For Second Lieutenant	CHARLES SHIELDS

Any further nominations may be made at the meeting.

Traditional events begin

When World War I ended in 1918, the club began an exciting period of rowing and swimming competition, becoming well known throughout the country. The celebrations, as the club took top trophies in races, led to social events — some of which continue today.

Social events at the club reflected San Diego life in the 1920s and 1930s. It was in this period that many of the traditional activities began: smokers, when the men gathered, the luaus on Brennan Island, and the regattas when everyone crowded the boathouse porches.

The January 1 Dip, first begun in 1892,[15] was meant to demonstrate "that swimming can be as much enjoyed in winter as in summer...." The members would jump into the bay from the boathouse or pier. Only once did they go elsewhere — to Mission Bay in 1925, where they were part of the holiday fiesta. The dip, which would last a few minutes or more depending on the fortitude of the member, was followed by a bowl of the San Diego Rowing Club's famous chili. The custom continues today, uninterrupted through the years. It is a significant unifying factor in the club.

San Diego Rowing Club

Presents

A LUAU (Native Feast)

Place—Brennan Isle

Time—Saturday Night, July 23, 1938

Dancing—9 p.m. Until ?

Feast—Native Style, 12 Midnite

Costume—
Ladies to wear Slacks
or Grass Skirts
Men in Whites or Go Native

Hawaiian Entertainment

$2.00 a couple—Positively no stags

Dancing—Eats—Entertainment—Swimming
Boating

52

66

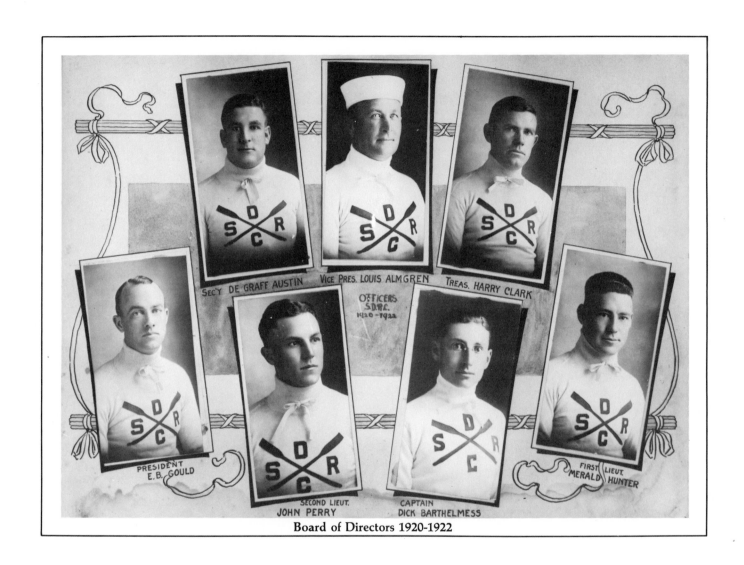

SEC'Y DE GRAFF AUSTIN   VICE PRES. LOUIS ALMGREN   TREAS. HARRY CLARK

OFFICERS S.D.R.C. 1920-1922

PRESIDENT E. B. GOULD

SECOND LIEUT. JOHN PERRY

CAPTAIN DICK BARTHELMESS

FIRST LIEUT. MERALD HUNTER

Board of Directors 1920-1922

Post-World War II change

After World War II, the club changed as San Diego had changed. The sobering years of concern with national safety, when there was fear of invasion and the city put out its lights, contrasted with the earlier carefree days. San Diego was not to return to those lighthearted days, and the club similarly lost four vital years. Membership, however, continued high after the war ended. In 1947, there were over 1,300 members.

Problems with lease negotiations concerned the club in the 1950s, and the sporting competition slowed. The clubhouse began to deteriorate; the members hesitated to repair it as the future was uncertain. It was the end of an era, for the Club could not return to what it had been.

R. D. Spicer and Neil Brown

In 1958, President DeGraff Austin reported:

With all our good financial record, our club is in the doldrums. It is natural to ask — why this slip downward in club affairs? My own feeling is:

1. *A new kind of club has come into being since World War II.*
2. *San Diego Rowing Club hasn't met this challenge while trying to do business as always in its present plant.*
3. *The parking situation at this location is bad, deteriorating, and being adjacent to a main traffic artery is not likely to get better.*
4. *The present club plant is not close enough to the residential area of the city as it once was. It is definitely located out at the end of a limb.*

In June 1972, the club's Tideland Use permit expired and they were placed on a month-to-month rental lease. In the late 1970s the club considered moving to a site on the newly created Embarcadero Marina Park which would surround the clubhouse. Contact with the Save Our Heritage Organisation in 1975 resulted in their support for the perpetuation of the building. It was again a difficult time for the club as lease negotiations were tentative and the club could not raise the money to build.

JAN 1st 1948

SAN DIEGO ROWING CLUB — BOARD OF DIRECTORS — ANNUAL MEETING 1946

DON BORTHWICK, PRES.   WM. WATTS, CAPTAIN   PHIL NEAL, TREAS.   GEORGE COOGER
     JOHN BUCKHOLDER, 1ST LIEUT.   KEARNEY JOHNSTON, 2ND LIEUT.   VICE-PRES.
                         DE GRACE WHITE, SECY.

Preserving the clubhouse

The San Diego Rowing Club has moved to small quarters in Mission Bay . . . and starts over, away from San Diego Bay, which was their home for ninety-one years.

The San Diegans For The Rowing Clubhouse, Inc., a group of preservationists and members of the rowing club, was created in 1980 for the sole purpose of retaining the building on site. Earlier appearances before the State Historical Resources Commission had certified the historical and architectural significance of the building.

This group appeared before the State Coastal Commission and the Unified Port District with Patrick Goddard, executive vice-president of Chart House Inc., in their efforts to save the building. Their arguments were successful, and in June 1983 the boathouse began a new era as a Chart House Restaurant.

January 1 Dip 1969

Dedication Day, January 1, 1900

Next to their shells and wherries, oars and smooth water, the clubhouse is the most important thing to the rowers. It is their identity, a physical evidence of their existence. It is a communal meeting place for club business and social activities, where they keep their boats, where they play handball, cards, wrestle, have lunch, sunbathe and talk. The boathouse is the focus of the membership, important because they cannot exist without it.

The first home

The first home for the San Diego Rowing Club was at Steadman's old boathouse, and it was probably these quarters that the club decided to buy, as announced in their third meeting. A bit premature, however, for within six months Steadman had resigned from the club, the club would move its quarters, and would instigate a lawsuit against Steadman.

Many committees were formed in the first meetings: constitution, bylaws, election of officers, and the purchase of boats. The one that received the least attention was their home, for they believed that Steadman's boathouse would be it. In the January 1889 meeting, it was suggested that they purchase it for $150; a month earlier, Steadman had offered to sell it for $250.[16] Some of the members wanted to buy; some wanted to go elsewhere. After a "large and enthusiastic" meeting on January 1, Steadman withdrew his offer to sell and resigned. The members proposed a move to Patterson's Sail Loft on D Street and the meeting broke up with bitter words. Within a week a court battle began with the filing of the initial documents.

Steadman complained that the nine rowing boats with oars and the raft were not the possession of the club because the plaintiff, J. L. Mathewson, president of the club, did not appear to be a "member of a volunteer association."[17] The club was not incorporated, hence had no legal identity. Steadman argued too that the club owed him monies and that the boats were being held because of this; the argument was clouded with ambiguous allegations.

Almost a year later, by court order in December 1889, Steadman was ordered to turn over the club's property to them. In 1900 a newspaper account would tell that Steadman's boathouse, the club's first home, was "blown away some years earlier."[18] (By this time, the club had its own "permanent" facility, but they were to be in two other places in between.)

H. FOETBROOK

The club moves

Their second home was the D Street boathouse, on Atlantic between E and D Street. They would stay here until 1891, changing the boathouse to suit their needs: a double door installed for the boat launching by trolley, a dressing room, lockers, and a fitted gymnasium. Realizing again that the boathouse was not quite adequate, a committee was formed to plan for the future. They suggested issuing shares in the amount of $5,000, with $3,000 allocated for the construction of a boathouse and $2,000 for equipment. The time had come, a member said, to "take decisive action to bring itself before the public and to enlist the support of the business men of the community."

To become a functioning club, the members reasoned, they needed the inducements of a clubhouse and "ample accommodations for athletic sports"; more than rowing was needed to bring in the men who might be past the prime of rowing age.

"This club is now laboring under difficulties which would be entirely overcome if better quarters could be obtained," Judge Aitken said. And another said, "The more the subject is discussed among the business men the more do they incline to it, because it recommends itself at once to their intelligence as wholly practicable and one of the best things that could happen to the city."[19] Also, they said, it would lead to a series of aquatic exhibitions and would be a good advertisement for the city.

Many suggestions were discussed during the meetings, and an architect was hired in 1890 to design a floating boathouse. It was to be such that it could be towed "to any point of the bay to accommodate any occasion. It (would) contain a billiard room, a dining room and a private dressing room,"[20] — an interestingly grand boathouse for a little club that would continue to have problems for some time.

It was a time "fraught with important consequences to the club" and "political matters," and these had to be dealt with. The October 1891 failure of the California National Bank ended the hopes of building, for it affected subscribers who could not now honor those subscriptions. The members decided to move back to the steamship wharf (although not to Steadman's boathouse) where the water was deeper, allowing for easier launching of the boats.

... And moves again

It was on July 11, 1891, that the club signed a lease with L. A. Chandler, and the "first building on the right going out" would lodge them until 1900. The parties agreed that Chandler would improve the premises and that the club would advance the monies which would be translated into rent credits.

Always aware of their need for a permanent home, the club wisely stipulated that it could "remove to other quarters" if need be, but that the monies would be forfeited, if any indeed remained. The rent would be $15 per month, ending in 1894, and the sum they advanced was $270.[21] They located on the "southerly side of the wharf of the Pacific Coast Steamship Company about midway between the outer end and the shore end of said wharf...." President E. J. Louis in his 1892 report stated that "... no member has reason to feel ashamed of our present home and facilities."[22]

The club had much larger quarters, a 20 x 45-foot building with its improvements of showers, lockers and more boat storage. There was a wide porch for sunning, a good launching ramp by a divided float, diving boards and a pole to show the depth of the water.[23] The years of disorganization appeared to be over and the club entered into an era of growth.

Building committees were again appointed, for the club wanted its own boathouse, and more bonds were issued,[24] for the earlier subscriptions had been used in the improvements of Chandler's boathouse. They had several options: 1) they could

San Diego Rowing Club 1908

buy the Chandler boathouse for $1,000, but Chandler wanted $1,400; or 2) they could buy and move the Coronado bath house — which seemed to be a desirable choice, for with a floor laid over the 60 x 30-foot swimming tank and a roof built over it, it would give a large central boatroom more than twice the size they now had. Also, it had 72 dressing rooms. The club was prepared to place the house on lighters and move it across the bay.

But again, those plans did not work. They chose a third option, to build their own boathouse, one designed to their needs and specifications. No longer would they adjust their needs to someone else's property.

A home at last

They decided they had enough money to build, and the first pilings were driven on November 9, 1899, by Captain Polhemus. They had moved just 250 feet south of Chandler's and would share the steamship wharf. They would remain here for almost 79 years.

Thirty piles were driven, the building resting on 24 of them. It measured 82 x 59 feet (with a veranda 70 x 6 feet), giving them about four times the space they had before. An observation platform extended above the peaked roof, commanding, they reported, "one of the finest views in the city." The club pennant (four flags each with a letter S-D-R-C) and the American flag flew from the platform.

A room was set aside for the use of the ladies' crews; it had ten dressing rooms and shower-bath.[25] One side of the clubhouse was to be devoted to the women, "separating them completely from the side of the house devoted to men ...," a token, for the club began and remained until recently "a man's club." The boatroom was 45 x 30 (and sometimes 40) feet with sliding doors. The men's quarters had dressing rooms, showers, sun porch and sports equipment.

A formal housewarming was held on January 1, 1900. The signal flags were used as drapery around the veranda, the pennant was flying and the house was decorated with flowers, palms, smilax and plants. Tea was served in the front ladies' quarters and punch was in the office area. Two hundred of the members came, bringing their friends to admire the boathouse. The main boatroom, they pointed out, would function as a fine dancing floor with canvas stretched over it.

Fifteen members dived into the 58-degree water on their annual January 1 dip. The clubhouse was everything they needed and wanted in a boathouse. At last they had a home. But within a few years, about the time that the subscriptions were paid off, they were again considering where they should move.

John Forward diving from club roof

STROKEOAR
WITH APOLOGIES TO BARTHELMESS

San Diego Rowing Club's Annual Dip
New Year's Day, 1915, at 12:30

The Directors request you to be present at this dip, as moving pictures will be taken which will **be** shown throughout the country, and no better advertisement of our climate can be obtained than **by** a picture of this kind flashed on the screens of almost every Theatre in the land.

J. W. Fisher

Anderson Borthwick

Louis Almgren, left; Alonzo D. Jessop, right

1911 Champion Team

O. J. Stough, 87 years old,
Jan. 1 Dip 1915

Problems again

Two problems consistently bothered the club members: the sewage condition and the leases, first with the steamship company and later with the port district. These problems would continue to concern them through seven decades and would ultimately result in another move which would be the last.

Through the years, many committees were organized to "find a home" for the club. In 1919, a motion was carried that a "New Club Fund" be created with not less than fifteen percent of the dues collected to be set aside for this fund.[26] Also in 1919, they discussed merging with the Yacht Club; plans were even drawn in anticipation of this merger. At this time, the old wharf that had been built in 1869 was wrecked and a new wharf was constructed to the boathouse.[27]

By 1923, there was talk of taking advantage of the Mission Beach offer made by the Spreckels Company.[28] "Everyone present" agreed it was a "proposition too good to let slide." It was speculated that Spreckels might even give them a long-term loan to finance the project and would bring a special express car service to the site if they would build there. It was decided that Mission Beach, however, was too far away and they decided against the move.

Many other proposals came. One, to combine with the San Diego Athletic Club, becoming the Mission Bay Branch of the main club, was again declined.[29]

By December 1924, President Harry S. Clark reported the gravity of the situation. A seawall, he reported, would be built along the United States bulkline, a 200-foot channel would be dredged, and the area shoreward would be reclaimed. The land would be leased by several large lumber companies. The club's lease, Clark added, would expire in 1949, but the city had reserved the right to use any portion of the leased land, which would result in the loss of the northerly wing of the boathouse and the boat landing. The club would then be 200 feet from shore with no wharf approach.

Talking to Architects

Two architectural sketches were presented for consideration. One, by W. Templeton Johnson, would cost from $75-85,000 to build. Club member Harry K. Vaughn, now an architect in Los Angeles, drew plans for a less expensive $60-79,000 design. The decision was made to relocate at the foot of Ash Street and to build the Vaughn design. It seemed a better decision than securing a location and building in the area where they were then located.

Along with these two alternatives, the club also considered moving to the Coronado shore. The special meeting called to examine the situation was argumentative — a clash of opinions. Two choices were argued: relocate to Ash Street in the area to be developed by the city for recreational purposes or remain on site and wait, for the lease stipulated that compensation was guaranteed if the city exercised its right to develop the tidelands.

A member of the committee urged that they wait. Commissioner J. W. Sefton of the Harbor Commission (and also a club member) vigorously argued that the club should relocate. The board members suggested a move to Ash Street.[30] A month later, the membership affirmed it by voting 304 for and 52 against. Two months later, it was decided to stay on site, for the harbor development was not definite and the club had no money.

But it was not over. At the annual meeting, the Building Committee reported that the Staniford Plan (the 1924-5 Harbor Development Plan) defined South Bay as industrial and the northern area, Cedar to Laurel Streets, as recreational. The club was located in the industrial area, undesirable.

Where to move?

There were five desirable locations to be considered:
— *in the immediate vicinity of the present clubhouse — not, however, permanent;*
— *at La Playa with ample ground and facilities but considered too far from downtown;*
— *in the Harbor Redevelopment area between Cedar and Laurel Streets, ideal except that a wide boulevard would pass between the shore and the clubhouse;*
— *on a recreational pier to be extended into the bay in the vicinity of Cedar Street — but to be built in the distant future;*
— *or at a location on the proposed Battery Park site near the ferry service.*

San Diego Rowing Club Rowers

The Battery Park site was decided to be the best, on smooth water and near town, and it was here they opted to relocate. Max Winter, a member from the earliest days, was asked to do a preliminary sketch for a clubhouse, one costing not more than $30,000 to build.

Six months later, the club learned that the Harbor Commission felt that the club was asking for land considered too valuable for recreational use. In October 1927 Captain W. P. Cronan of the Harbor Commission told the club that "at the present time, there seemed to be no place along the waterfront available for the club."[31]

In June 1927, it was decided that the clubhouse be made "... ship-shape for a period until a new clubhouse on an appropriate site becomes more of a possibility."

Even though they wouldn't move until 1979, plans continued for a suitable home. In 1927, the club considered Market Street; in 1930, Atlantic Street, where they submitted sketches showing a $70,000 house having club rooms, boat-room, gymnasium, dining room, four handball courts, sun-bathing room, an outdoor swimming tank and two tennis courts.

✮ **SDRC PRESIDENTS** ✮

Year	President	Year	President
1888	J. E. Peterson; H. R. Larrison; J. G. Decatur	1931-1936	J. W. Fisher
1889	J. L. Matheson	1937-1941	Harley E. Knox
1890	R. K. Holmes	1942-1946	Anderson Borthwick
1891	E. J. Louis	1947	Philip M. Neal
1892	W. R. Rogers	1948	George E. Courser
1893-1900	Dr. T. J. McConkey	1949-1951	A. Elmer Jansen
1901-1907	J. S. Akerman	1952	William G. Watts
1908-1911	James Wadham	1953	William S. Petry
1912	Alonzo Jessop	1954	Louis Almgren
1913-1914	Charles E. Sumner	1955-1957	H. DeGraff Austin
1915	Max Winter	1958-1959	Clyde Davee
1916	I. L. Leszynsky	1960-1961	Harlan Torkelson
1917	Milton H. Epstein	1962	Charles Morgan
1918	James E. Wadham	1963	Jim Martinos
1919	Charles E. Sumner	1964-1971	Percy Rooks
1920-1922	E. B. Gould	1972-1974	Richard Stout
1923	Louis Almgren	1975	Bob Schumake
1924	Harry S. Clark	1976	Eugene Rague
1925-1926	Edgar A. Luce	1977-1979	Jerome Navarra
1927-1930	Louis Almgren	1980-1983	Gary Thomas

✮ ✮

Brennan Island

Changes did occur, and in 1934 an island was created from the dredging of the bay. Through Port Director Joe W. Brennan, a club member, the club leased the island, and in 1937 a handball court was built, satisfying the need for two regulation courts.

Brennan's Island was dedicated in May 1934, a 150 x 450-foot island located about 200 yards southeast of the clubhouse with a catwalk joining the two. It was planted with palm trees and flowers; horseshoe pits, badminton courts, volleyball courts and sandboxes were added. The handball court building was used until 1979 when it was demolished and the island was incorporated into the 1978 Embarcadero Marina Park.

Once again in 1934, even as Brennan's Island was being created, the club voted to apply for the Battery Park site, ". . . as soon as the attitude of the Board of Harbor Commissioners is learned."[32] At the same time, possibly now aware of the instability of harbor plans, they repaired the boathouse and applied to the port for a fifty-year extension of their lease at one dollar per month. The lease wasn't granted as requested, but a site was being held on Battery Park, the club members were informed.

In December 1942, the lease was finally concluded: a fifteen-year extension from 1949 (when the existing lease would expire) at a fee of one dollar per month. This lease also included Brennan Island. [33]

Brennan Island from air

Handball Court Building

Mission Bay

In 1946, Mission Bay development began, and the club considered applying for a site there. It might be better, they reasoned, to be out of the constant uncertainty of bay development and be part of the purely recreational attitude of Mission Bay.

In 1952, a site at Shelter Island — a 400 x 250-foot area where they would have their own beach, parking, a building with docks, floats, etc. — was a viable consideration, and President Elmer Jansen warned, "I personally feel that a club must go forward or slide down hill." There was the problem of attracting a younger crowd, for the club was no longer getting them as members. The club was in danger of becoming a sun-bathing club. Rowing and swimming, the backbone of the club, were declining.

Change was necessary, regardless of the nostalgia that each member felt for the location. Another building fund was started and another building committee appointed. During the 1950s, Mission Bay plans continued.

In 1952, President Elmer Janson again warned:
An organization can't survive if it just stands still, you must either advance or fall back ... new members must constantly be obtained or we'll start on the downgrade as older members drop out or die.... We must look ahead. We must adopt a widened family type program to interest members, their families and friends. We haven't those facilities at the old club, but there'd be a beach at the new place.

The membership voted to move, and drawings were again presented, by architect Louis Bodmer. In 1959, with still no new home, President Clyde Davee reported in the annual message:

We are in a dangerous period where a few months of complete indifference can kill our 73-year-old club. We need member interest, prompt payment of dues and charges and a desire to have those fine people we know share our love for SDRC and to obtain active members.... I recommend that we do our best here and plan for a move to new shores and a new plant. We must work for a continuation of the club we love so that countless young men of the future may have the mental, moral and physical aid in growing up that you and I have had.

In 1962, George Courser objected: "Maybe I'm of the old school and influenced by fondness for tradition, but I'm against moving.... Haven't we been successful enough where we are? A family club might increase the membership, but it would be a different club altogether and might cause some of the old standbys to lose interest entirely." Llano Briggs objected to Courser's remarks, saying they were "... rapidly becoming an old man's club.... We need new blood to carry on...."

In the early 1960s the club was seriously negotiating with the city for a Mission Bay site. The most appropriate, they believed, was on the east shore in the vicinity of Tecolote Creek. A financial plan was established and the details were finally agreed upon. It would be on a four-acre site, a 22,000-square-foot building in the colors as approved by the Mission Bay Commission. In February 1962, however, President Harlan B. Torkelson said:

> In closing out my two years as president, I would like to be able to say that we have a lease signed at Mission Bay, and that we were well on our way to having a new club, but it is impossible to say. It isn't because your Board of Directors did not try. I do feel though, that all the arduous leg work has been done and that now your new Board of Directors elected tonight will be able to consummate the lease with the city this year and we will be able to get started.

Harbor Development

By 1970, the club had a year-to-year lease with the port and once again the development plans were influential to the club's future. With the development of the Embarcadero Marina Park, the club would be forced to relocate, as the present site would be surrounded by land and the area used for work boats.

Negotiations continued for an 8.3-acre site near the San Diego Flood Channel on Mission Bay. The negotiations were conducted in the name of San Diego Aquatic and Recreation Club — the title selected to describe the club's function and activity. A million-dollar facility having a boathouse, a minimum of six handball courts, twelve tennis courts, an Olympic size pool, showers, lockers, saunas and gymnasium was designed.

"We must move"

In 1972, outgoing President Percy Rooks again warned the membership at the annual meeting:

> The survival and perpetuation of the San Diego Rowing Club have been paramount in my thoughts over the last number of years; this concern is strongest and most acute at this particular time for we are at the crossroads of a decision which resolves simply into two unavoidable alternatives: (1) whether we are disposed to just stand by and watch this venerable and honorable old club die or (2) whether we wish to continue its existence through our collective support of and/or affiliation with the San Diego Aquatic and Recreation Club. It is rumored that various of our members have expressed the desire to remain at this present location. Believe me, I would like to, also, and I possibly have a stronger motivation than the majority of those people, for I am now in my forty-fifth year as a member, but I know it is not possible. . . .

Seven years later, in 1979, the club did finally move to Mission Bay. It was not a grand million-dollar facility, nor did they merge or change their name. They moved to a small facility in the Santa Clara Recreation building. President Jerry Navarra closed the door of the old boathouse. He had led the last efforts to remain, but continuing lease disagreements, notification of fire violations, and the deterioration of the building finally led to the closing of the clubhouse.

The club applied for historic site designation for the clubhouse, and in July 1975 it was designated Site No. 105 by the San Diego Historical Site Board. On August 30, 1979, it was placed on the National Register of Historic Places.

Brennan Island Picnic

SPORTS

The Crew Classic held in 1982 used an appropriate quote from Oliver Wendell Holmes which he gave at the Yale Commencement in 1886:

> *Why endure long months of pain in preparation*
> *for a fierce half-hour that will leave you all but*
> *dead? Does anyone ask the question? Is there*
> *anyone who would not go through all its costs,*
> *and more, for the moment when anguish breaks*
> *into triumph . . . or even for the glory of having*
> *nobly lost?*

Holmes asked the question: "Is it worth it?" To the rower, yes. For competition is personal and inherent in the oarsman and winning or losing is a product of it. The rower competes with a fellow rower or a team or just the water and shell itself. Kearney Johnston, an oarsman for fifty-three years, rows each day. He enjoys "making the boat run," testing his ability just a little more to see if he can go just a bit farther, a little faster.

Johnston is only one of the hundreds of champions who have rowed for the club in national and international contests. They have won trophies and medals for the club, affirming that it was the "ruling power in club rowing in California," for many years.[34]

Kearney Johnston - Winner of a gold medal at the International Veteran's Rowing Regatta at Bern, Switzerland, in 1974

Light Weight Crew: D. Beekley; S. Foushee; B. Edmonds; A. Borthwick; unknown; B. Fontaine

Rowing

Sportsmanship was a hallmark of the club, among the members and in the races. In an early event, a competing team from Vancouver, B.C., reported:

> ... *Permission was at once asked to allow us to cut the coxswain's seat back the proper distance, thereby making a much better boat, but after pressing all week for this privilege, we were finally refused.... The arrival of the San Diego contingent fully vindicated the stand we had taken, for we found that they had made the very alteration we desired in both their shells! And it is both just and appropriate to record that those very fine sportsmen represented by Capt. Knox and Directors Laidlow and Barthelmess at once and in the most sporting manner conceivable, offered us the choice of their shells.... While deeply appreciating such a splendid and notable tribute to true sportsmanship we could not handicap these fine chaps, who had we accepted their generous offer, would have been left with only one shell to row their three races in....*[35]

The club won this Pacific Coast championship, "another notable triumph for the San Diego crew ... [however] these same fine sportsmen from San Diego were generous enough to express the opinion that had the Vancouver crew been equally boated they would have won...."

It was the attitude in the last part of the nineteenth century and into the twentieth that exercise was health-giving.

In 1899, Dr. T. G. McConkey (who was president of the club from 1893-1900) wrote of the "importance of outdoor exercise ... to correct the sedative effects of our very equable climate."[36] "Nothing," he claimed "was of greater value than a combination of a hard row on the bay followed immediately by a short plunge and swim in the cold water of the bay...."

The first regatta

Within weeks of organization, the club had appointed a committee to arrange a regatta, and this was held for Admission Day on September 10, 1888. Twenty-five hundred people gathered to watch the eight rowing events. The seventh event was a single scull race between a Mr. Schmidt and W. J. Peterson for the amateur championship of San Diego. Peterson won by "nearly two seconds."

The race was not without humor. The eighth event was a double scull race manned by T. Haines and A. Ashton against the single scull of David Dean. It ended with Haines and Ashton swimming ashore, tugging their "treacherous craft" behind them. It seemed the scull "leaked badly" and slowly sank into the water, leaving the rowers no choice but to dive into the bay. Dean, however, had "everything his way" and stopped often to "let the double scull catch up."[37]

A tub race was probably the most comical event, as almost all the tubs sank before they were three feet from the float. Two, however, managed to go the distance to victory, being "rowed or rather towed" by the rowers.

The afternoon events this 1888 day were a success and "spoke volumes" for the club. So successful were they that on Thanksgiving Day, two months later, they staged another regatta with two single scull races, a four-oared race, a Grand Four oared race for the championship of Southern California, and a Grand Handicap when "the entire fleet entered, manned promiscuously."

Recognition and honors

Regattas and competition became an important part of club life in the years before World War II. The club competed for the western coast championship through the Pacific Amateur Association, rowing against Vancouver and Victoria, British Columbia, and against San Francisco, Alameda, and Long Beach. They competed nationally against the Philadelphia and Chicago teams in the National Association of Amateur Oarsmen. (Today, the club is a member of the United States Rowing Association.)

The era before World War II is considered the golden years, exciting times, for the club consistently trained good oarsmen and competed in many races — and generally took top honors. Welcome home parties became a part of the social life of the club and the city, for the newspapers headlined the victories.

Among the champion oarsmen who rowed for the club in this time were A. Wharton Coggeshall (called by many "the greatest oarsman I've ever seen"), C. Arnholt Smith, E. B. Gould, Kearney Johnston, Willard Hage, Harley Knox, Andy Borthwick, Del Beekley, Joe Sefton, Joe Jessop, Sr., Charlie Lentz, DeGraff Austin and Charlie Springer.[38]

Competing for the Olympics

The club competed in several Olympic finals. In July 1928, the team consisting of Charlie Springer (stroke), Herb Henschel (No. 3), DeGraff Austin (No. 2), A. Wharton Coggeshall (bow) and Del Beekley (coxswain), with J. W. Fisher and Harley Knox as coaches, competed in Philadelphia to qualify as the American representative to Amsterdam in August 1928.[39] The team made the finals, but lost to Harvard by two seconds.

In 1932, the same team again reached the finals with Bob Hampton replacing DeGraff Austin as No. 2.[40]

The club supported their Olympic teams, and in 1932 the gabooners wired their best wishes: "Just figure every fellow on the sun porch this bright noon has a hold on that oar too." The worst opponent for the team (and one they had feared) was the humidity. That, along with the "moving water" (choppy), contributed to their defeat. They lost to Penn Athletic Club by three lengths. In 1956, the club team was again affected by the humidity and didn't place in the finals.

But in 1964 Jim Storm, a club rower since his high school days, won an Olympic Silver Medal for Double Sculling with partner Seymour Crowell.

Regattas after the war

In 1948, after a wartime hiatus, a Spring Regatta was again begun and other events were sponsored, although not in the numbers and scope of the pre-war years. The club competed on the west coast, still a strong contender, and winning as before.

The club now schedules two events a year: a spring and a fall championship. The races are open to all west coast oarsmen and are held on Mission Bay.

Jim Storm, Olympic Winner 1968

Olympic Team 1932

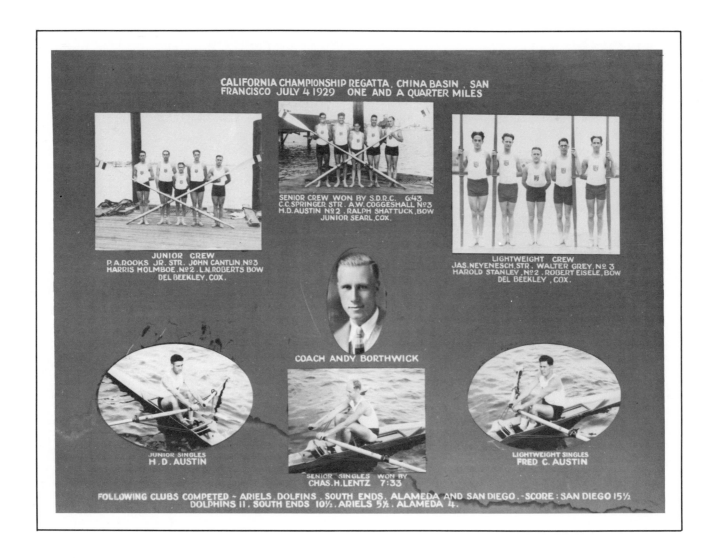

CALIFORNIA CHAMPIONSHIP REGATTA, CHINA BASIN, SAN
FRANCISCO JULY 4 1929 ONE AND A QUARTER MILES

SENIOR CREW WON BY S.D.R.C. 6:43
C.C.SPRINGER STR. A.W. COGGESHALL No3
H.D.AUSTIN No2 . RALPH SHATTUCK, BOW
JUNIOR SEARL, COX.

JUNIOR CREW
P.A.ROOKS JR. STR. JOHN CANTLIN, No3
HARRIS HOLMBOE, No2 . L.N.ROBERTS BOW
DEL BEEKLEY, COX.

LIGHTWEIGHT CREW
JAS.NEYENESCH, STR. WALTER GREY, No 3
HAROLD STANLEY, No2 . ROBERT EISELE, BOW
DEL BEEKLEY, COX.

COACH ANDY BORTHWICK

JUNIOR SINGLES
H.D. AUSTIN

SENIOR SINGLES WON BY
CHAS.H.LENTZ 7:33

LIGHTWEIGHT SINGLES
FRED C. AUSTIN

FOLLOWING CLUBS COMPETED - ARIELS, DOLFINS, SOUTH ENDS, ALAMEDA AND SAN DIEGO. - SCORE: SAN DIEGO 15½
DOLPHINS 11, SOUTH ENDS 10½, ARIELS 5½, ALAMEDA 4.

Collegiate rowing

The San Diego Rowing Club has always felt a responsibility toward the teaching of rowing, and has extended its facilities and coaching abilities to the local universities, to junior oarsmen, and to the Sea Scouts branch of the Boy Scouts. Through Del Beekley, who has long advocated collegiate affiliation with the club, and Kearney Johnston, many young oarsmen have learned the skill of rowing and many have become championship rowers.

The future of rowing lies in the high school athletes, many of the club members believe. And it may be here that the future of the club also lies. An aggressive program by the club will serve the community and will make the club a vital part of the rowing renaissance that is beginning today.

Swimming

The 1888 club regatta also included swimming, for this was considered a year-round sport in San Diego. The club promoted swimming with its January 1 Dip. It was called the "jolliest crowd [and] emphasized the worth of living."

The first swimming course in the 1888 regatta was set from R. B. Steadman's float to a point near the east end of the steamship wharf and return. No starting gun was used, just a loud "Go!" — and the eight contestants disappeared under the water. The first official winner of a club race was F. D. Weston, ten feet ahead of all the rest.

Swimming continued to be a lasting and vital part of the club. Each year, the club participated in statewide meets and usually won. Swimming was a major sport factor before and after World War II, although its emphasis today has declined.

Earl "Esther Williams" Kyle felt that swimming was the superior sport offered by the club and so debated in 1953:

> *The sport of rowing is a fine exercise for strong back and shoulder muscles, also to develop hard, knotty legs and thigh muscles similar to the mighty oak tree type and large fannies from sliding back and forth, pulling on a long piece of wood, called an oar. Now consider the sport of swimming. This sport calls for smooth, rippling, flowing type of muscle, that makes for perfection of movement and precision of action in propelling the body through the water.... Think of the wonderful picture a fish makes, gliding along without apparent effort and then try to think of a jellyfish trying to compete in such a performance.*[41]

San Diego Rowing Club 1979

John Neyenesch

Hector Rivera and Kearney Johnston,
1950 Skeeters Doubles Champions

Auten Pease

C. Arnholt Smith

A. Wharton Coggeshall

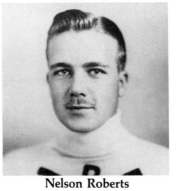

Nelson Roberts

F. R. Kelly

In 1901, Wilbur Kyle had challenged H. F. Brewer, the champion swimmer of the United States, to meet him at the club and defend his title. It was no championship match, the club knew, but a club member's competing against Brewer (even on an informal basis) would be prestige enough. Kyle was a superior swimmer and did give Brewer a severe challenge, but could not beat him. It was significant, however, for the course was fully surveyed and timed and both swimmers established a world's record for the quarter mile.[42]

President Akerman told the club of the race:

> *Had it not been for the efforts of some of the officers and directors of the club, Brewer would not have come to San Diego, the course would not have been measured and the amateur athletic association would not have allowed and established his record. . . .*

In 1920, Clarence Pinkston won an Olympic medal for high diving. Swimming champions Claude Clavert, Charles Shields, Ed Herzog, Junior Dula, Earl Kyle, George Bean, Dick and George Jessop and Ray and Bill Spicer are among the great swimmers of the club who consistently represented it well in championship meets.[43]

Claude Clavert, Ed Herzog, Charles Shields

W. F. Sutor, Founder of Skeeter Club

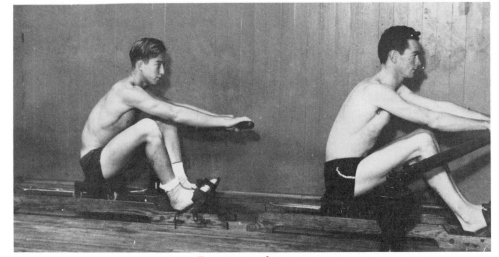

Rowing machine

SUB-CLUBS OF THE SAN DIEGO ROWING CLUB

Name	Organized	Qualifications	Purpose
Vikings	1907	Win or coach a winning team in state championship	Recognize state champions
Skeeters	1913	Row a distance of 1½ miles in less than 9½ minutes	Promote and teach art of sculling
Dolphins	1914	Swimming prescribed course in forty minutes	Develop interest in long distance swimming
Piledrivers	1918	Rowing a wherry around the skeeter course	For younger members
Old Timers Club	pre-1935	Members of continuous twenty-five years	Meet and visit with rowing buddies of twenty-five years
21 Club	1950	Any handball member of the club who has won a Club Handball Championship	Promote and teach the art of handball
Century Club	1960	Member of rowing club	Financial assistance to club

H. FOETBROOK

TOURNAMENTS AWARDS TO SAN DIEGO ROWING CLUB

Name	Year	Qualifying	Type
Admiral Line	1939	Emblematic of the most exasperating oarsman	Trophy
Arnold, Charles E.	1927-1942	Most valuable oarsman	Trophy
Athletic Club Regatta	1906	4-oared shell, Los Angeles	Trophy
Baranov Doubles		Bowling	Trophy
Baranov, Nate		Horseshoes — Class A Doubles	Trophy
Beacon 12	1946-1953	Swimming prescribed course	Trophy
Borthwick, Andy	1949-1977	"Bull throwers"	Trophy
Borthwick Perpetual	1934	Emblematic of club championship in handball	Plaque
Bowling	1941;1946	Bowling	Trophy
Buchanan Cup	1927	Canadian Cup	Trophy
Canoers	1946	Bowling	Trophy
Coronado Cup	1907	Junior Four	Trophy
Coronado Tent City		Transbay Swim	Plaque
Coronado Tent City	1912	Canoe tilting	Trophy
Dolphins	1914-1916	Five-mile swimming	Medal
Epstein, Milton H.	1916	Skeeters Doubles	Trophy
Handball Challenge	1951;1952	Handball	Trophy
Handicap	1948;1953	Swimming	Trophy
Jessop Coast Champions	1936	Emblematic of a Coast Championship	Trophy
Jessop, George Carter	1911	Beacon 12 Swimming	Trophy
Jessop		Horseshoes	Trophy
Killiefish	1914-1948	Bronze, Silver and Gold	Medal
Knights of Columbus	1936;1937	Oceanside Pier Swim	Trophy
Labor Day Roughwater	1933	Oceanside — swimming	Trophy
Marathon Swim	1946	Swimming	Trophy

National Rough Water	1936-1941	Swimming	Trophy
PAAO Silver Cup	1914	Rowing	Trophy
Pacific Beach Swim	1938	Swimming	Trophy
Peterson, Henry C.		Senior Singles Sculls	Trophy
Pile Driver Champion	1929	Roy Tharaldson; Time 14:37-2/5	Trophy
Regatta, Spring	1914;1952;1953	Senior single sculling	Trophy
Rife	1932-1946	Single sculling excellence	Trophy
Rogers Cup	1914	Senior four-oared champions	Trophy
San Diego Sun Trophy	1905	Rowing	Trophy
San Diego Rowing Club		Handball	Trophy
San Diego Rowing Club	1913	Rowing barge	Trophy
San Diego Rowing Club	1944	Bowling	Plaque
Senior Barge	1913		Trophy
Silver Gate Channel	1912-1929	Swimming marathon	Trophy
Spellman, Wm. R.		Best time on Skeeter course by novice	Trophy
Springer	1915;1915;1951	Swimming	Trophy
Senior Four-oared Shells	1908	Naples, Nov. 26, 1908	Trophy
Sungold			Trophy
Steinman	1941		Trophy
Tent City Swim	1926	Swimming	Medal
Tide Pole Handicap	1947	Swimming	Trophy
Tower Bowl	1941;1945;1946	Bowling	Trophy
Towne, Ben, Perpetual	1940		Trophy
Trompas	1956	Handball	Trophy
Union Oil Dock	1935-1952	Swimming — R. D. Spicer	Trophy
Wilson, Wm. M.		Amateur oarsman	Trophy

(Note: this is a partial list, and dates are provided where available.)

BOY SCOUTS OF AMERICA

CHARTERED BY CONGRESS JUNE 15, 1916

CHARTER

GRANTED TO

THE SAN DIEGO ROWING CLUB

upon its proper application through its duly authorized representative to carry on the Senior Scout Program for

CHARACTER BUILDING : CITIZENSHIP TRAINING

subject to the provisions of the Constitution and By-Laws and rules and regulations of the National Council of the Boy Scouts of America for one year.

SEA SCOUT SHIP

#594, SAN DIEGO, CALIF.

SHIP COMMITTEE

W. G. WATTS, CHM'N. DE GRAFF AUSTIN
LEROY THARALDSON DR. W. T. SAYRE-SMITH

J. W. BRENNAN

SKIPPER

EUGENE M. STORM

MATES

DONALD GRANT CHAS. B. DE LONG, JR.

These officials have been duly certified and are officially registered by the National Council to meet the responsibilities of their respective offices in accordance with the provisions of the Constitution and By-Laws of the Boy Scouts of America.

IN TESTIMONY WHEREOF the National Council has caused this charter to be signed by its officers and its corporate seal to be affixed.

DATED
DECEMBER 31, 1946
49

For fifty-seven years beginning in November 1926, the club has sponsored the Sea Explorer Ship #294. (It has also been known as #594 and #2294.) There have been only two skippers: Eugene Storm (1926-1963) and Steve Hulbert (1963-present). The Explorer ship was quartered on the Star of India from 1926-1961 while it was berthed near the club. From 1961-1979, the troop was quartered on Brennan's Island.

★ ★

Handball

Handball began locally at the club in 1902. Until they moved to Mission Bay in 1979 where there are no handball courts, the members actively participated in games and championship meets.

Handball was considered an especially effective conditioning exercise for rowers, and interest in the sport never declined. It was the most popular sport in the winter months when rowing activity slowed.

Tournaments in handball measured the competitive abilities of the members; they began in 1914 and continued until the late 1970s.

Many members reached distinction both locally and nationally. Just a few of the champions were E. B. Gould, Neil Brown (who was Club secretary from 1903-1917), Merald Hunter, George and Dick Jessop, Caesar Pastore, Charlie Weldon, Junior Todd, Bish Edmonds, Andy Borthwick and Alex Trompas.[44]

Handball Team: H. Cohen; N. Roberts; B. Edmonds; G. Parkinson (Mgr.); F. Manning; A. Feinberg; W. Peterson

Horseshoe playing on Brennan Island

Bowling began in 1922

Basketball began in 1935

Newspaper coverage

The club received good coverage through Rowing Club newspaper columns throughout its years of existence. From 1925 through 1942, Dick Barthelmess, a member and officer of the club, wrote a daily *San Diego Sun* article, "Rowing Club Gossip." (This column had appeared before 1913 without name credit.) Other columns, also specifically about the club, were "The Clubites" (1940-1942), "Rowing Club Splashes" by Clyde Davee (1947-1950), the "Rowing Club Tales" by Harold M. Dill (1949-50) and the "Rowing Clubites Corner" by DeGraff Austin (1942). These columns appeared both in the morning and evening papers on a daily basis.

Other shorter-term columns also ran, and the newspaper coverage very thoroughly reported both the social and the sporting activity of the club members. The club members also had their own internal newsletters. The most popular was the "Red and White Log."

★ ★

Rules of the Excelsior Rowing and Swimming Club

The Excelsior rowing and swimming club is now the most prosperous athletic organization in the city. Their boathouse, adjoining the steamship wharf, is kept in good condition, and the members are governed by the following rules:

1. Members returning from a rowing trip must leave the key to the boathouse with R. H. Steadman.

2. No boat belonging to the club shall be left made fast to the lighter.

3. Members returning with any club boat must wipe the boat outside and inside and place her on the racks in ship shape style.

4. All members using boats shall make the proper entries in the log book.

5. Non-members are not permitted to use any club boats.

6. No member shall use the property of another member without his permission.

7. The boathouse must be cleaned, oars properly placed in the racks, seats placed in the boats, and everything left in a neat condition by all members after using boats.

8. Any damage to any club boat must be recorded in the log book and reported to the captain.

9. All members will see to it personally that no dogs are allowed to use the boathouse as a bath house.

10. No outside boats will be permitted to tie up at the lighter unless they be those of visitors to the boathouse.

11. No vulgar or profane language will be permitted in the clubhouse.

12. Any departure from these rules will be subject to fine.

San Diego Union
7-30-1888:1:5

44

ROWING CLUB MEMORIES

There are memories here, the big and small things that happened at the boathouse, on the road, in the shells, at restaurants, at parties, during competition — with each other and against each other — anywhere and for any reason. They are remembered with nostalgia and chuckles and they are part of the story of the club.

The memories are shared by the thousands who have been club members since it began decades ago. They are typical San Diegans, yet different, and like other clubs' members but still not the same. They are concerned with exercise, friendship, competition and having fun.

Their memories are the small happenings, some having meaning only to them. They talk about how much this member would eat, for there were always "rowing club eating stories." They laugh when remembering the coxswains who were thrown into the water after each race, traditionally, for the coxswain always "got a free ride." They talk of towing the wood out to Brennan's Island for the lanai and recall that some of it sank in the bay.

They tell of getting lost in the famous San Diego Bay fog, sometimes spending the night on a buoy. They agree that Del Beekley would make it home without bumping into something because of his "magnetic attraction" for home base.

Not all of the rowers experienced what Al Bernardini did, but they could have. During a race, the sliding seat of the shell came loose. Instead of stopping the race, Al slid back and forth on the rails. By the time it was over, he was quite bruised, and his team members, wanting to help him, reached for the oil but got the turpentine instead. Al, for one, still remembers it.

The rowers are just not the same as other athletes, President Gary Thomas points out. There is a mystique that is hard to define. "A rower will get up before dawn," he said, "will launch his shell in knee-deep icy water, row an hour or so, then wash and dry his shell and be back home before the city is awake. How can you understand someone like that?"

They are rowers. They joined the club because it gave them a place to row, because they wanted to exercise. They stayed because they enjoyed it, they made friends, and maybe most of all, it was their club.

H. FORTBROOK

Jay Mellusi was named "Great Lover for 1938" in the club; he succeeded William Watts who was getting married.

The Rowing Club Man

OFFICIAL PUBLICATION OF THE SAN DIEGO ROWING CLUB
Entered at Postoffice, San Diego, California, as Second Class Matter
Issued on the First of Each Month

Vol. I	MAY, 1918	No. 1

"HELLO, CHARLEY!"

ROWING CLUB FOLK have always been noted for their wonderful hospitality. They have always given the glad hand freely and gone more than half way toward making the stranger within the sacred bounds of the sun parlors "at home."

Our up-and-at-'em section, just 116 strong, have joined the colors, and it's up to each man who remains "behind," to assist in fostering the grand ol' spirit and give the "Hello Charley" with a ring, to fellow clubsters at all hours.

This little act costs nothing and goes a long way in the direction of a better, brighter and more attractive S. D. R. C.

So let's give the ol' smile, folks, and keep the famous greeting a-going full force—it pays.

Rowing Club Tales by Harold W. Dill
(San Diego Union, May 27, 1950)

Tomorrow morning at 10 the Club's Annual Spring Regatta will be staged off Brennan Isle with competition in seniors and lightweight divisions plus a singles race between three of our fastest skeeters. There will be motorboats supplied for members' convenience in viewing all stages of the races, according to Club Capt. Llano Briggs.

The 1950 swimming season gets underway in 2 weeks with the annual Marathon Swim starting June 10. Rebuilt turning boards are to be placed on the 50 meter course off Brennan Isle.

There will be three competitive divisions composed of Classes A, B and C which are based upon the number of lengths completed in the 5-minute time limit. A large turnout is expected for this good conditioning event which lasts through July 16 and will include such names as Rollie Thomas, Dick Torkelson, Bill Watts, George Eisele, John Monte-pagano, and Llano Briggs plus the old standbys Oscar La Branche, Spike Spicer, Chubby Shields, and Harold Dill.

It is the purpose of this swim to condition the club swimmers for the distance swims that are an annual event here since 1911 when the first Beacon No. 12 swim was held with George Jessop as the first title holder. This year the first swim on the calendar will be the Union Oil Dock Swim July 2. It was inaugurated by Charles Shields in 1930 and won that year by Edgerton Scott.

Sun Deck Chatter . . . Harry Bates is all set up for a 4-day fishing trip and according to Fred Rose, he is as nervous as a new bride about it. . . . Bill Spicer will be back in the swimming ranks again this summer after a year's absence. Chuck Morgan and Harlan Torkelson baited Harold Dill and Bill Page for two games in the small courts and then moved in for the kill during the third game which was no contest. . . . Sol Lowenfeld only had time for 15 or 16 shuffle board games with Elmer Jansen as he had to get back uptown last Sunday. . . . Carl Anderson, Sol Lowenfeld handball combination wasn't tough enough to beat the Llano Briggs, Dick Buel team for three straight games in the small courts.

In 1958, fifty years after they had won The Pacific Coast Rowing Championship, "Gerry" Baldwin, "Ed" Dodge, "Lonnie" Hackelman, and "Dick" Jessop met at the Old Timer's Club for a reunion and another row on the bay.

In the late 1930's, the SDRC had a dance at the San Diego Yacht Club which was at Coronado on Glorietta Bay. I was one of the hosts and during the dance was kidnapped and taken nearly to Imperial Beach and dumped out. I walked two-thirds of the way back before I was rescued by kindly rowing club members. (Kearney Johnston)

Back in the 20s, a unique form of amusement for some of us was to ride the swells behind the Coronado ferry paddle wheels in a canoe. One Sunday morning with George Poole in the bow, I in the stern, cut in on a swell between the paddle wheel and stern of the ferry so close that a brace between the hull and deck hit George's head which frightened him to the extent that I was in the dog house for several weeks. (Del Beekley)

Every time the club would get a new Boatkeeper, he would gather the old boat parts and tools which had been thrown in the bay under the club by the last Boatkeeper. He would wait for a very low tide to get them and clean them up for use. (Kearney Johnston)

Do you remember the annual Water Melon Feed that was held on the Coronado Strand?

Do you know how many rowing club members spent the night on one buoy or another? It seems that everyone did, but got to shore one way or the other eventually.

They were the Rowing Club boys, according to the San Diego Union in 1947: James Keller (District Attorney), DeGraff Austin (Chairman of the Board of Supervisors), Harley E. Knox (Mayor), Jean F. DuPaul (City Attorney). "The Rowing Club Boys now pull together in the development of the city," the article said.

Do you remember "Swineggle" — the pig that Fred S. Hage presented to the club in 1914? He proposed that the animal which he had won at a club Wild West Smoker be adopted as the official mascot and as such be named after the "renowned rowing crew." Not getting much response, Hage later demanded to know if the club intended to castrate Swineggle or barbecue him.

One night around midnight while waiting at Fourth and Broadway and much to my surprise, I saw Dick Barthelmess and a couple of out of town gentlemen friends wading and cavorting in the Plaza fountain. (Del Beekley)

Do you remember the trouble with the fish and birds while rowing? It seems that Kearney Johnston was torpedoed and wounded by a pelican and Buzz Austin was attacked by a porpoise which tried to get into the boat with him. Wise rowers would bang the oars on the water to scare the porpoises away. And do you remember when there was a $50 bounty on stingrays?

49

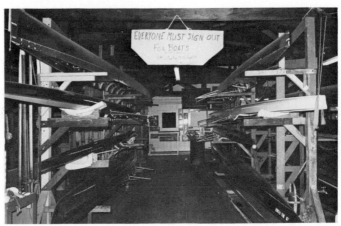

SAN DIEGO ROWING CLUB SCRAPBOOK

NEW MEMORIES. . . .

There is a boat slung under the boathouse canopy today. When club members first saw it, they recognized it as their old eight-oared training boat and decided maybe it would be great to use it again. Pat Goddard, John Callahan and John Creed (president of Chart House Inc.) smiled and told the story of the boat's relocation.

Stored away and ignored for some thirty years in a B Street warehouse, it had been brought out to add color to the new restaurant, enhancing the theme of a rowing club. The old paint was scraped off; new fiberglass was put on. It was painted white with a red stripe and it looked spectacular, just like new.

A hint of trouble, however, came when the crane began to lift the boat into place under the canopy. It bent in the middle, the ends rising perilously. Quickly, it was lowered into the water, for it was going to fall and would be lost forever at the bottom of the bay.

With John Creed in the boat using a single oar, and Pat Goddard in the water pushing and paddling behind, and John Callahan with a broom and someone else on deck with a line, they guided it onto some boards and very carefully held it in place.

Some weeks later, they patched it up again, repainted the worn spots, and secured it from within. It was anchored in place under the canopy. It still looks spectacular and if club members or anyone else cares to row it on the bay, they are welcome. Everyone else declines to go with them but John Creed will loan them his single oar. One stipulation, though: it must be returned, in proper condition, to the place where it is now.

In the spring of 1983, just before the clubhouse opened as the Chart House restaurant, an old-time member happened by and asked where the holes in the sundeck were. . .? It seems the carpenters, in the process of restoring the boathouse, had replaced the "damaged" boards. The old gabooners (those respected community members who would sun on the deck each day *sans* suits — solving all the problems of the world, but not local politics or private business, for that was understood to be taboo!) used those holes as the need arose, and if they were to return today, would be much distressed to see that part of club history gone!

The Chart House Restaurant 1983

NEW BEGINNINGS: ONE HUNDRED YEARS LATER

They are starting over. The club has moved away from where it was born ninety-five years ago, away from its home of seventy-nine years and in another bay. The little red clubhouse has a new owner and a new use. The steamship wharf is gone. It is a different time and a new era begins. But the two, the club and the clubhouse, are bound together and will remain so, for they share too many memories to be separate.

The club

The San Diego Rowing Club has survived to enter its second century. Theirs was a difficult birth, a giddy popularity and then a declining interest. Relocated and growing, the club is part of San Diego rowing today.

The club has survived because of its members — the rowers and the leaders. The rowers have always been there, for rowing is the reason that the club was created and the reason that it continues. The leaders have been there, too, refusing to let the club end. They have guided it in both the good and the troubled times.

Rowing competition today is focused in the San Diego Crew Classic, which is primarily for collegiate rowing and was begun in 1973. This annual event, with its thousands of spectators (in this basically non-spectator sport) is a significant part of the rebirth of rowing popularity. In the 1983 event, the club presented the Anderson Borthwick Trophy for the "Open 8" in memory of Borthwick's long affiliation with the club.

A new clubhouse is to be built and will retain the sense of "welcomeness" that permeated the old clubhouse. It was a bit ramshackle and rustic, perhaps, but it was comfortable to its members. It holds their memories. The new clubhouse will have that same sense of history, for their pictures and memorabilia, shared with the little clubhouse on steamship wharf, are of the past and form a bridge between that past and the present.

"The club spirit," President Gary Thomas said, "is still here." They are beginning a junior rowing program, Thomas said, for the champions of tomorrow are in the high schools today. The club's spring and fall regattas continue. A series of informal regattas on Friday evenings is being initiated. In their new location, the club will again be a leader in rowing.

Gary Thomas

The clubhouse today

The Clubhouse

The clubhouse is beginning again. In mid-June 1983, with parties similar to its Dedication Day, January 1, 1900, the doors were opened to guests. The old pictures are on the wall. Trophies and memorabilia are in the entryway. The shells are slung under the canopy as they were in 1900. The windows open onto the sun porch and flags fly from the observation deck. There is a sense of starting over, but the atmosphere is still San Diego Rowing Club.

In the 1970s, it didn't seem that the clubhouse would remain, for in the development of the harbor this area was allocated for workboat storage. Through the efforts of the San Diegans For The Rowing Clubhouse Inc., a preservation group formed for the purpose of retaining the boathouse on site, and Patrick Goddard of The Chart House Inc., the clubhouse was recognized as an historical element and allowed to remain.

Goddard had approached the club in 1977. He was interested in restoring the clubhouse as a restaurant, he said, but only if the club could not stay there. He wrote his name on the back of manager George Stephenson's card, and asked to be contacted if the club had to give up their clubhouse.

It was two years before Goddard was to join with the preservationists. By then, the club had relocated and the demolition of the building had been mandated. The restoration credits of The Chart House Inc. were a factor in the saving of the boathouse. This organization has recycled a considerable number of historic buildings, many of them award-winning. In early 1981, their restoration plans for the clubhouse were approved by the Port Commission.

And so the clubhouse starts again, restored almost to its original look. It becomes a part of the new harbor life of San Diego.

★ ★

SAN DIEGO ROWING CLUB
525 EAST HARBOR DR., SAN DIEGO, CALIF. 92101

GEORGE STEPHENSON
MANAGER

PHONE
232-1898

PAT GODDARD
V.P. DEVELOPMENT
CHART HOUSE RESTAURANTS

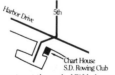

San Diego Rowing Club

The Board of Directors is pleased

to invite you to the Club's

1983 Annual Christmas Party,

on Friday, the sixteenth of December,

at six o'clock, at the boathouse,

on Santa Clara Point, Mission Bay.

Catered hor d'oeuvre,   *Please RSVP,*
no-host bar   *297-6341*

EPILOGUE

By the 1970s, it seemed that neither the San Diego Rowing Club nor its boathouse would survive. The club's membership was down to a few hundred, and most of these were handball players. There was a desperate need for money to repair the boathouse, meet lease requirements, and to replace the rowing equipment.

The controversy about their location — an argument of so many decades — was taking all of the club's energies and was seriously complicating the financial situation. By 1978, there was no choice left and the club was forced to close its doors and move to Mission Bay.

The move, however, brought about a cohesion that had been lacking for some years. Efforts became focused on reorganizing the rowing competition, improving the equipment, increasing membership, and establishing goals for the future. A new site was chosen for the clubhouse (one that will be more than just a boathouse), and the club is targeting a 1988 move-in which will coincide with their centennial.

The boathouse also suffered in the 1970s. By 1980, the abandoned building was breaking apart on the bay. Parts floated in the water and washed against the pilings, damaging them even further. Little hope remained that it could be saved. But the rapid deterioration of the building and the ramifications of its loss spurred the San Diegans For The Rowing Clubhouse, Inc., to intensify their efforts, and the Unified Port Commission finally supported a lease request by the Chart House Inc. Within two years, the boathouse was restored and has become one of San Diego's most popular restaurants.

The club is now a viable part of San Diego rowing and of the aquatic world on Mission Bay. The spirit that held it together from its very beginning is evident, and club members know where they are going again. The boathouse, as part of the new San Diego Bay development which is more oriented to visitor use, is also secure in its new identity.

The club and the boathouse have separated, each beginning a new phase. They were perhaps not always good for each other, for the factionalism that arose out of its site location adversely affected both. They are compatible again, as they were in the beginning, divided only by distance, and each is happy in its new life.

SAN DIEGANS FOR
THE ROWING CLUBHOUSE, INC.

President: Patricia Schaelchlin
Vice-President: Henry Roloff
Treasurer: Carol Lindemulder
Secretary: Glen MacNary
                  Robert Peck
                  Robert Sjogren
                  Gary Thomas
                  George Stephenson
                  Leonard Wolf

The San Diegans For The Rowing Clubhouse, Inc., was organized in early 1980 and received its incorporation papers in March 1980. Its sole purpose was to preserve the San Diego Rowing Club boathouse on its original site.

The group consisted of members of the San Diego Rowing Club, the Save Our Heritage Organisation, and concerned San Diego citizens. They appeared before the member cities of the Unified Port District for resolutions of support, and before both the San Diego Unified Port Commission and the California Coastal Commission. They received support from the political, cultural and organizational community.

In June 1980, the Chart House Inc. joined with the San Diegans For The Rowing Clubhouse, Inc. This liaison brought the financial support needed, and with the 1983 restoration and re-use of the boathouse, the San Diegans For The Rowing Clubhouse, Inc., disbanded.

San Diego Rowing Club
Spring Championships — 1983

The San Diego Rowing Club will hold its 1983 Spring Champion-
ships Regatta:

Date:	Sunday, April 17th
Time:	7:00 AM - 1:00 PM (Registration & lightweight weigh-in at 6:30 AM)
Location:	Mission Bay Course (off Santa Clara Point)
Distance:	1000 meters

The first race will start at 7:00 AM; subsequent races will
begin every 15 minutes thereafter. The order of events shall
be posted and announcements mailed to each entrant prior to
race day. If an event is scratched, the schedule may advance;
however, the order will remain fixed and consideration will
be given to maintaining reasonable rest periods between
linked events. Flexibility will be stressed and an attempt
will be made to include any event and/or class for which
three or more entries are received.

Entry fees are $5.00 per person unlimited number of events.
The entry fee for a race in a pair, four, double or eight is
$3.00 per person (coxswains ride free). Awards for 1st, 2nd
and 3rd places will be presented following the last race.
SDRC invites competitors and their beach crews to a picnic
starting after the races. We'll provide sandwich makings and
soft drinks; we don't guarantee they will last!

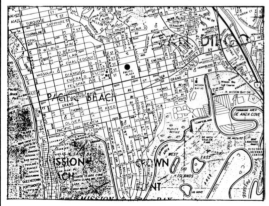

Please com-
plete the
entry and
mail with
entry fees
to:

Galen Justice-Black
2826 Canon Street
San Diego, Calif.
92106

Please return
entries no
later than
April 13th.

On January 1, 1984, for the ninety-second time, the San Diego
Rowing Club members had their annual dip in San Diego Bay.
Chart House Inc. made the boathouse available to them for both
the dip and the traditional club chili. For a while, it was the rowing
club home again. At 5:30, the Chart House at the Rowing Club
opened the doors for restaurant business and the club members
returned to their home on Mission Bay.

"A man doesn't realize what life means until he has tasted a little of our club life."
Pres. Alonzo D. Jessop, May 13, 1913

FOOTNOTES

1. *San Diego Union* 5-28-1887:5:2

2. *San Diego Union* 1-1-1892

3. *San Diego Union* 6-8-1888:5:2

4. Articles of Incorporation, Club Records

5. *San Diego Union* 2-22-1881

6. Barthelmess, Richard, "The Clubhouse on Steamwhip Wharf," in *San Diego Historical Quarterly*, October 1960, Vol. VI, No. 4

7. September 30, 1893

8. *San Diego Union* 6-6-1895:5:2

9. Club Records

10. Minutes 5-15-1922

11. *The Rowing Club Man* 1919

12. Minutes 8-27-1942

13. Minutes 11-6-1945

14. Minutes 7-21-1942

15. *San Diego Union* 1-1-1892 and *San Diego Union* 1-1-1938

16. *San Diego Union* 1-1-1889:9:2

17. Superior Court Record #2860, San Diego County Court House

18. *San Diego Union* 1-2-1900:6:2

19. *San Diego Union* 9-27-1890

20. *San Diego Union* 8-29-1890

21. Club Records

22. *Ibid.*

23. *San Diego Union* 7-31-1891

24. *San Diego Union* 7-21-1899:6:4

25. *San Diego Union* 10-11-1899:7:1

26. Minutes 5-8-1919

27. Minutes 10-7-1920

28. Minutes 11-22-1923

29. Minutes 9-26-1924

30. Minutes 3-12-1925

31. Minutes 10-25-1927

32. Minutes 2-25-1937

33. Minutes 12-18-1942

34. *San Diego Union* 6-24-1931; "This N That" by Ted Steinman

35. *Vancouver Province* 9-12-1925; "Southenders Lacking Fine Spirit of Sportsmanship"

36. *San Diego Union*, 11-5-1899

37. *San Diego Union* 9-11-1888

38. Refer to *San Diego Rowing Club 1888-1947* (Club Records) for a comprehensive list of champion oarsmen for this time period.

39. *Tribune* 8-13-1927

40. Club Records Scrap Books

41. Club Records

42. *San Diego Union* 1-1-1902:17:5-6

43. Refer to *San Diego Rowing Club 1888-1947* (Club Records) for a comprehensive list of champion swimmers for this time period.

44. Refer to *San Diego Rowing Club 1888-1947* (Club Records) for a comprehensive list of champion handball players for this time period.

BIBLIOGRAPHY

The records of the San Diego Rowing Club have been used as the principal source for *The Little Clubhouse on Steamship Wharf.* These records consist of the minutes from 1913 to the present, log books, file records (correspondence, membership, inventories, sub-clubs, maintenance, etc.), scrapbooks, and interviews with members of the club. *The San Diego Union* newspaper files of the San Diego Public Library and the University of California-San Diego from 1880 through the present provided information regarding the formation and evolution of the club. These newspaper records were also used to trace the regattas and sports competition that the club engaged in. The litigation records of 1889 were researched through the Old Records at the San Diego County Courthouse. Topical folders at both the San Diego Public Library and the San Diego Historical Society were used.

The San Diego Rowing Club records have been placed in the San Diego Historical Society archives and are available for research purposes.

The pictures are from the collection of the San Diego Rowing Club with the exception of pages vi, 12, 14, 20, 30, and 51, which are from the San Diego Historical Society-Ticor Collection. Sketches on pages 3, 22, and 29 are by Heather Fortbrook.

INDEX